BOOK ON RELIGIOUS EXERCISE AND QUIET

St. Isaiah the Solitary

Translated by: D.P. Curtin

Dalcassian
Publishing
Company

PHILADELPHIA, PA

ISBN: 978-1-960069-63-4 (Paperback)

Library of Congress Control Number:
Author: Curtin, D.P. (1985-)

Book design by J.J. Ripplestick

Printed by Ingram Content Group, 1 Ingram Blvd, La Vergne, Tennessee

First printing edition 2023.

I. There are three virtues which always contribute to the mind: natural impetuousness, fortitude, and the great length of vitality.

II. There are three virtues which, if the mind sees in itself, it is confident that it has reached immortality: discretion in all things, and distinguishing adroitly the great variety of vices, one from another. I foretold that all things should be completed early in the morning, and the firmness of the mind is greater compared to one that allows itself to be persuaded by another's words.

III. There are three virtues which always give light to the mind, to whom they are present: not knowing the malice of any man, bearing the coming of things undisturbed, and the drive not to be sinful. These three, in turn, give birth to three others that are greater: not knowing the malice of man begets charity. In short, not seeing evil brings peace.

IV. There are four virtues which punish the soul: silence, keeping the commandments, living narrowly, and feeling low about oneself.

V. Isaiah said the same thing: "I see myself as a wandering horse, having no master. He who finds me sits on me, and after he had let me go to another, occupying me in the same way, wanders off.

VI. Take care not to be caught in those things in which you have sinned before, so that old sins are not renewed within you. Be humble, and that humility will protect you from your sins. Give your heart to obey your fathers, and the grace of God will dwell in you. Do not be wise in yourself, swollen with your own opinions, and do not fall into the hands of your enemies. Accustom your tongue to speak while the words signify agreement, and humility will come upon you. Dwelling in your cell, take care of these three matters: industry, meditation, and prayer. Consider every day: "We have this day to work in this world, whether I shall have it tomorrow, I do not know". By doing so, you do not sin twice against God.

VII. Do not indulge in gluttony in repast, lest your former sins be renewed in you. Do not be distracted in any work, lest the violent attacks of the enemy fall upon you. Give yourself strength to act vigorously while at prayer, and the rest of God will come to you quickly. Force your hand to many prayers with tears, and perhaps God will have mercy on you and strip you of the old sinful man.

VIII. Work, begging, and traveling, and tolerance of the hard life and the life of silence, give birth to humility; and humility forgives all sin.

IX. If sexual lust attacks you, afflict yourself without ceasing in vigilance, in hunger and thirst, in humility towards all things. Yet, if the beauty of the body and the imagination of pleasure with a woman draw your heart, remember the smell of these, and you will rest.

X. Do not, brother, as long as you are in this life, give rest to your body, and do not trust in yourself if you see yourself struck by the tumult of melancholy; for the demons restrain their power by cunning for a time, and when a man has negligently relinquished the secure interest of his salvation, they suddenly spring upon the wretched mother of his soul, and snatch her away like a sparrow. If they happen to overcome it of their own volition, they mercilessly cast down all that sin. Let us stand therefore in the fear of God, and let us guard ourselves, carrying out perfectly all the works of our religious discipline, and exercising all the virtues suitable to ward off the impiety of these things. Indeed, the labors and struggles of this short time not only preserve us from guilt, but prepare the crowns of the soul before it leaves the body. As many as have the seal of holy baptism, let us endeavor to forsake our sins, that we may find mercy on the day of judgment. Let us contend, dearly beloved, since the time is at hand. Blessed, therefore, is he who is always engaged in this anxiety in his mind, day and night alike.

XI. It is necessary to ward off the attack of the evil demon from the heart by pious contradiction at the time of prayer, lest we find ourselves speaking to God with our lips, but thinking absurd things in our hearts. For God does not accept from a sacred man who makes empty and mocking prayers to you. For everywhere in the Scriptures it is contended that we should guard the senses of the soul, for if the will of the monk is submitted to the law of God, and according to its law he governs all his subjects. They say this of animal motions, especially anger and concupiscence, since these are subject to reason. They work virtue and do justice, especially turning the desire of pursuing God and his mind. Yet, inciting anger against the devil and sin can proceed. What is required next then? Hidden prayer.

XII. When standing from the opposite side against a crowd of enemies, you see them fleeing back from you weakened, do not give your heart joy, because the malice of these spirits feeds them. They will, of course, prepare the battle more vigorously than before, placing troops in ambushes outside the city, and ordering them to continue there unmoved, so that, in the meantime intending an attack, and fleeing from your encounter again, they may drive you out of the city with the fervent confidence of their first success, through this act, beyond the hidden ambushes.

XIII. Our Master Jesus Christ, knowing the great mercilessness of our enemies, and the cruelty of the human race, commanded against the bitterness of heart, saying: "Be ready at every hour, for you do not know at what hour the thief comes. Let it not happen that he should come and find you sleeping." And again he said: "Take care that your hearts are not weighed down by debauchery, and drunkenness, and worldly cares, and suddenly judged." Stand therefore upon your heart, paying attention to these senses, and if the memory of God has peace with you, you will apprehend the thieves who plunder it. For he who watches the thoughts exactly, discerns which of them, by their entering, attempt to pollute him. For they disturb the mind, so that it may not feel that it is a fraud, either to help others, or to be restrained by laziness. Those who know their own cunning remain undisturbed, making requests of the Lord.

XIV. If your soul wanders, and you do not know how to restrain it, your activity of willing and unwillingness draws it to wander. For unless Gideon had broken the jars, he would not have seen the light of the lamp. Thus, unless a man despises the body, he will not see the light of divinity.

XV. When a city is besieged by the hands of another, if any part of the wall is breached, the enemy, when they attack, will pay attention to that breach in order to enter through it. For although the guards are ready at the gates, they will not be able to resist the enemy unless this destruction is avoided. Thus a monk, who has some weakness for women, no matter how hard he tries, he will never be able to reach the goal of perfection.

XVI. Scrutinize yourself, brother, every day deeply examining and searching your heart, whether there are any faults in it in the sight of God. Cast out whatever is from him, lest the occasion of evil should come upon you from that point. Therefore take heed to your heart, and watch over your enemies. Indeed, they are cunning and swift in their malice. Direct your heart to what I am about to say: "it is impossible for him who does evil to do good." For this reason our Savior taught us to be vigilant, saying: "Narrow is the gate and narrow is the way that leads to such a power; and there are only a few who find it."

XVII. Take care, therefore, that no perdition leads you away from the charity of God. Keep your heart, and do not be troubled, saying: "How can I keep my heart, when I am a sinner?" For when a man forsakes his iniquity and turns himself to God, his repentance regenerates him into a whole new, unchangeable creation.

XVIII. A monk must persevere constantly in the religious struggle of training, and be careful to guard against the attacks of the adversary; and therefore, like a sailor, he must pass through the waves, obeying the divine grace at the helm, never deviating from the right path. But to pay attention to himself alone, and to address God in peace of mind, unbending in thought, and secure in the mind of all other things.

XIX. I exhort you not, while you are in the body, to relax your heart from anxiety about your safety. For the farmer cannot have certain confidence that the grain which he sees already born in his field will lead to a happy outcome. For he does not know what will happen to him before the harvest. Then, finally, he is safe when he has stored the wheat that has already been cleaned in his barns. So a man need not worry about loosening his heart, as long as the spirit is in his nostrils. It is not right for a monk to be absolutely sure of his perseverance and safety before he has breathed his last. Therefore, he must always cry out to God, imploring his help and mercy. Some adversities will befall him, because of previous impiety he has suffered such misfortunes.

Migne's Latin translation (1863)

I. Tres virtutes sunt menti providentes semper. naturalis impetus, fortitudo, et impigra strea nuitas .

II. Tres virtutes sunt quas si mens apud se viderit, confidit pervenisse se ad immortalitatem: discretio, subtiliter ab invicem discernens species diversas vitiorum; provisio cuncta præcogno scere mature occupans; et firmitas animi nun quam persuaderi sibi sinentis id quod aliena cogitatio suggerit.

III. Tres virtutes sunt quæ semper lucem suppe ditant menti cui adsunt: nescire malitiam cujusvis hominis; supervenientia ferre imperturbate; et be nefacere maleficis. Hæ tres porro istæ tres alias gi gnunt se majores: nescire malitiam hominis gignit charitatem: ferre supervenientia imperturbate af fert mansuetudinem; denique benefacere maleficia affert pacemi.

IV. Quatuor virtutes sunt quæ castificant ani mam: silentium, custodia mandatorum, anguste habitare, et humiliter de se sentire.

V. Dixit idem Isaias: Video me ipsum ut equum errantem, non habentem dominum, et qui eum invenit sedet supra illum; et postquam is eum dimiserit, alius eumdem similiter occupans, inscendit.

VI. Custodi te ipsum ne captiveris in iis in quibus alias peccasti, ne peccata vetera renoventur in te. Auna humilitasem, et illa te proteget a peccatis tuis. Da cor tuum ad obediendum patribus tuis, et gratia Dei habitabit in te . Ne sis apud teipsum opinione tui tumida sapiens, ne incidas in manus hostium tuorum. Assuefac linguam tuam ad loquen dum verba consensum significantia , et humilitas ve niet super te. Residens in tua cellula trium sem per horum curam gere: laboris manuum, meditationis et orationis . Quotidie reputa : Hunc diem habemus ad operandum in hoc mundo, an crastinum habiturus sim, nescio. Sic faciens, non pecca bis in Deum.

VII. Ne gule indulgeas in refectione , ut non renoventur in te priora tua peccata. Ne attedieris in aliquo labore, ut non ingruant in te vehementes insultus inimici. Vim infer tibi ipsi ad strenue agen dum in meditatione tua, et veniet in te requics Dei velociter. Coge te ipsum ad multas orationes cum fletu, et forte miserebitur tui Deus, et exuet te veteri homine peccatore.

VIII. Labor, et mendicitas, et peregrinatio, et tolerantia durorum, et silentium, pariunt humilitatem. Humilitas autem remittit omne peccatum.

IX. Si fornicatio te impugnat, afflige te ipsum indesinenter in vigilia, in faune et siti , in humili tate ad omnes . Si vero pulchritudo corporis et ima ginatio voluptatis in femina trahit cor tuum, recordare fetoris istorum, et requiesces.

X. Noli, frater, quandiu fueris in hac vita, dare requiem tuo corpori , nec confidas in te ipso si te videris feriantem a pravorum affectuum tumultu; cohibent enim vim suam dæmones astu ad tempus, et cum homo negligenter securus studium suæ salutis remiserit, repente insiliunt in miseram ani mam, et rapiunt eam ut passerem. Ac si eam superare ipsis ex volo contigerit, ad omne illam peccatum immisericorditer dejiciunt. Stemus igitur in Dei timore, et custodiamus nos, exsequentes perfecte cuncta religiosæ nostræ disciplinæ opera, et exercentes omnes virtutes idoneas arcendæ ho stium improbitati. Labores quippe ac contentiones brevis hujus temporis, non modo præservant nos a culpis, sed coronas præparant animæ priusquam egrediatur e corpore. Quotquot habemus sancti baptismatis signaculum, studeamus relinquere peccata nostra, ut inveniamus misericordiam in die judicii. Contendamnus, dilectissimi, quoniam tempus prope est. Beatus ergo qui hanc semper animo sollicitudinem versat die pariter ac nocte

XI. Oportet appulsum mali dæmonis avertere a corde per piam contradictionem tempore orationis, ne quando reperiamur labiis quidem alloquen tes Deum, corde autem absurda cogitantes. Non enim acceptat Deus ab homine sacræe qui ti vacante orationem lutulentam, et irrisoriam. Ubique enim Scriptura animæe sensus ut custodiamus contesta tur, nam si subjiciatur voluntas monachi legi Dei, et secundum legem ejus gubernet subjecta sibi, omnes, inquam, animales motiones, præsertim au tem iram et concupiscentiam, hæc quippe subsunt rationi, virtutem operatur et justitiam facit, con cupiscentiam quidem ad Deum et ejus voluntates desiderandas vertens, iram autem contra diabolum et peccatum incitans. Quid autem deinceps requiritur? Occulta meditatio.

XII. Quando ex adverso stans contra turbam hostium, videris eam a te debilitatam retro fugere, ne cor tuum des lætitiæ, quoniam malitia spirituum istorum past ipsos est. Paramt scilicet bellum priore acrius, collocando turmas in insidiis extra civitatem, et jutendo ibi eas perstare immotas, ut, interim intentantes insultum, et tui rursus occursu fugientes, te fervide primi successus fiducia per sequentein extra civitatem eliciant ultra insidias latentes: quo cum imprudens perveneris, exsurgent in te a tergo cohortes insidiantes, et iis qui modo fugicbant, repente frontem vertentibus, circum venta in medio, et undique pulsata, infelix anima quo confugiat non habet.

XIII. Magister noster Jesus Christus sciens m guam hostium nostrorum immisericordiam, et mi seraus genus humanum, mandavit in amaritudine cordis dicens: Estote parati in omni hora quia nescitis qua hora fur venit. Ne forte veniat , et inve niat vos dormientes; et rursus ait: a Videte ne graventur corda vestra crapulis, et ebrietatibus, et curis sæcularibus, et superveniet vobis repente ho ra. Sta igitur super cor tuum, attendens tais sensibus, et si pacem tecum habuerit memoria Dei, comprehendes fures deprædantes ipsam. Qui enim exacte invigilat cogitationibus, discernens cognoscit, quænam ex iis ingressu tentent ut polluant ipsum: turbant enim mentem, ut illa vel alio iuten ta, vel desidia constricta, fraudem non sentiat. Al qui astutiam ipsorum norunt, imperturbati manent, postulantes a Domino.

XIV. Si anima tua vagetur, et tu nescias eam stringere, operatio tua volentis incertum in nolen tis, trahit eam ad vagandum. Nisi enim Gedeon confregisset hydrias, non vidisset lucem lampa dum. Sic nisi homo contemnat corpus , non videbit lumen divinitatis.

XV . Ut civitatis circumseptæ manibus si muri pars aliqua labem fecerit, hostes cum oppugnantes attendunt ad labem illam ut per eam introeant. Quamvis enim custodes ad portas præsto sint, ne queunt resistere hostibus nisi reparetur quod diru tum est. Sic monachus cui vitium aliquod domina. tur, quantumlibet conetur, uunquam ad perfectionis metain pertingere poterit.

XVI . Perscrutare te ipsum, frater, quotidie penitus intuens et pervidens cor tuum, ecquid in ipso vitiorum sit in conspectu Dei; et illud quidquid est ex ipso ejice, ne mali occasio inde veniat super te. Aute igitur cordi tuo, et vigil observa hostes tuos. Etenim astuti et vafri sunt in malitia ipsorum. Ac plane persuade cordi tuo, hoc quod mox dicam: fieri non posse ut qui male agit agat bene. Propter hoc docuit nos Salvator noster vigilare, dicens: Angusta porta et arcta via est quæ ducit ad vi tam; et pauci sunt qui inveniunt eam.

XVII . Attende igitur tibi, ne qua perditio abducat te a charitate Dei; et contine cor tuum, et ne attærdieris dicens: Quomodo possum cor custodire , cum peccator sim? Quando enim reliquerit homo peccata sua, et se couverterit ad Deum, poenitentia ejus regenerat ipsum, et totum in novam creatu ram immutal.

XVIII . Debet monachus perstare constanter in certamine religiosa exercitationis, et attendere ob servandis insultibus adversarii, et, ut nauclerus, fluclus pertransire, gubernaculo obsequens divinæ gratia, nusquam declinando a via recta. Sibi autem soli attendere, et in pace animi Deum alloqui, cogitatione indeflexa, et mente rerum cæterarum omnium secura.

XIX . Hortor te, ne, quandiu es in corpore, relaxes cor tuum a sollicitudine salutis tuæ; ut enim agricola non potest certam habere fiduciam proventuri ad felicem exitum fructus, quem jam natum in agro suo videt; non enim scit quid ei eventurum ante messem sit; ac tum demum securus est , quando triticum jam purgatum in suis horreis condidit: sic homo non debet cura solvere cor suum, quoad spiritus in naribus ejus est. Ac sicut homo quivis ante supremum anhelitum tenere se ipsum nequit quin in aliquod aliquando labatur vitiu: ita fas non est monacho ante ultimum anhelitum esse prorsus securo perseverantiæ ac salutis suæ. Sed oportet ipsum semper clamare ad Deum, implorando ejus auxilium et misericordiam. adversitates aliquas inciderint, ob antecedentem improbitatem infortunia ejusmodi subiisse.

Other Titles by D.P. Curtin:

First Book of Ethiopian Maccabees (2018)
Book on Religious Exercise and Quiet by Isaiah the Solitary (2022)
Vision of Theophilus by Cyril of Alexandria (2022)
On Fate (De Fato) by Albertus Magnus (2023)
Fragments of 'Chronicle' by Hippolytus of Thebes (2023)
Life of the Blessed Theotokos by Epiphanius Monachus (2023)
Syriac Life of John the Baptist by Serapion the Presbyter (2023)

www.ingramcontent.com/pod-product-compliance
Lightning Source LLC
Chambersburg PA
CBHW070959120626
46546CB00004B/1691

* 9 7 8 1 9 6 0 0 6 9 6 3 4 *